Cobweb's Sixt

Written by Daphne Faunce~Brown
Illustrated by Lynne Byrnes

For James and Nicolette

Published by Studio Publications (Ipswich) Limited.
32, Princes Street, Ipswich IP1 1RJ

AS Cobweb looked out of the window, his heart sank. Today was July 9th, his sixth birthday. He and Wellington had planned a picnic tea, but rain lashed down from heavy clouds and the wind howled.

Then Cobweb spotted Wellington struggling towards him with a big square parcel. His spirits rose.

He ran and opened the door to a very wet Wellington who wished him "Happy Birthday" and handed him the blue box.

Cobweb

Cobweb quickly opened it and inside he saw a brown rectangular box.

He opened this box only to find yet another. This third box was round and orange with a circle of green ribbon around the lid.

"How long does this go on for, Wellington?" asked Cobweb, enjoying the joke.

"That's all," said Wellington. "I know you like opening parcels so I used three boxes to make it last longer!"

Cobweb eagerly opened the last box but was rather disappointed to find that it held a ball of white string. Of course he didn't show his feelings.

“Thank you for taking so much trouble, Wellington. String is always useful.” Cobweb hoped Wellington would not see the large ball of string he already had on his mantelpiece!

"Goodbye for now, Cobweb," said Wellington cheerily. "Tea will be ready at three o'clock. Don't be late."

Poor Cobweb. Pouring rain and a ball of string. It was not a good start to his birthday. However, he knew that Wellington had invited Jasper Toad and the three young Tabbies, Thomas, Tarquin, and Clover to join them for tea and so he felt the day was bound to improve.

Cobweb was with Wellington in time to greet Jasper Toad at three o'clock.

Jasper loved wet weather and bounced in happily, handing Cobweb a dripping wet, oval-shaped parcel.

Cobweb quickly removed the yellow paper and, just as quickly, his heart sank, for all he found was a flat piece of shiny wood!

Fortunately for Cobweb, the three Tabbies arrived just at that moment and so he didn't have a chance to thank Jasper.

Drops of water flew in all directions as the Tabbies shook themselves. Unlike Jasper, they hated the rain.

Cobweb smiled bravely as he was wished "Happy Birthday" and handed a very long, green parcel.

He could hardly believe his eyes when he opened it, for it held three sticks and a roll of material!

Before he had the chance to feel even more down-hearted, everyone burst out laughing!

"I might have known it was all a joke," said Cobweb, "especially with you around, Wellington!"

The Tabbies quickly made their present into a large triangle. It was a grey wigwam with red and black patterns on it.

"Just right for a camping holiday," suggested Thomas. Cobweb was really pleased and thanked them very much.

COBWEB'S
HOUSE

Jasper surprised Cobweb by simply turning his present over. On the other side were the words "Cobweb's House" neatly carved in the wood.

"Jasper, you are kind and clever," said Cobweb. "As soon as it stops raining I shall fix it to my gate."

Then it was Wellington's turn. "You really do need more string, Cobweb," he said, "for this would be quite useless without it."

Then he handed him the most beautiful red and green diamond-shaped kite, something he knew Cobweb had always wanted.

Cobweb was thrilled to bits and very happy now.

When Cobweb blew out his six candles, he made a wish. It was for tomorrow to be dry but windy!

Cobweb's wish came true and he had so much fun when he flew his kite!